CANAL GUIDES

VENETIAN
DOMESTIC ARCHITECTURE

A GUIDE TO VENETIAN DOMESTIC ARCHITECTURE

"VENEZIA MINORE"
BY EGLE TRINCANATO

DISCOVERING THE LITTLE-KNOWN VENICE OF
THE "SESTIERI" OF CASTELLO AND DORSODURO
ILLUSTRATED BY 160 DRAWINGS OF BUILDINGS
FROM THE 12TH TO THE 18TH CENTURY

EDITED BY RENZO SALVADORI

CANAL & STAMPERIA EDITRICE
VENEZIA

ISBN 88-86502-10-9

CONTENTS

PREFACE

This pocket edition of "Venezia Minore" (Venetian Domestic Architecture) is being brought out just thirty years after the first edition, published in 1948 (*). It was high time, here as elsewhere, to turn our attention to the houses of ordinary people which make up the continuum of the city.

I am indebted to Renzo Salvadori who has taken on the task of revising this edition in the form of a guide book in which, even though the original text is shortened and the number of illustrations in the original is reduced, all the ninety examples in the 1948 edition are illustrated. The pocket edition is in a more convenient form, more economical in price, and therefore more accessible to a wider public; it also includes precise topographical indications which will be particularly useful to non-Venetians.

One of the reasons which prompted me to accept the editor's proposal (my hesitation was due to the fact that the study had not been brought up to date after so many years) was the fact that this domestic architecture in Venice is still an almost unknown face of the city, even though it forms its most authentic, vital feature, in the sense that it represents (or ought to represent) the Venice of the majority of its inhabitants. This domestic architecture is, in fact, the true nucleus, the heart of the problem of Venice. Far too many of these minor buildings are today abandoned or in conditions of extreme decay, while Venetians are forced to go elsewhere to find houses to live in - a phenomenon which is the main cause of that dramatic loss of vitality of the historic centre which we all know so well. It is my hope, therefore, that this small book may be helpful in the first place to Venetians, and to all those, both Italians or foreigners, who love our city, by helping them to get to know it, they will help us to defend it. Venice possesses the extraordinary quality, both aesthetic and social, of this domestic architecture which even today strikes us as being particularly modern.

Many of these buildings, including those erected by the Republic, that is by the Procuratoria, by guilds or charitable foundations, as part of a policy of social welfare established many centuries ago, were built with standardized methods, liberally interpreted, so that, beginning with modular elements (single windows, mullioned windows, balconies, dormer windows, chimneys on the façade, etc.) it was possible to create a wide variety of façades and ground plans.

The façades are always indicative of the interior plan, and by applying designs based on well-organised symmetry and a careful balance of proportions, we obtain architecture which is organic and rational at one and the same time. To this should be added the respect for the house as individual nucleus, expressed in providing, even in the humblest houses, independent staircases for each flat (nos. 10 ,28, 59, 67, 70, 79, 84), and the way in which each building is adapted to the urban structure, so that we find those semi-public, semi-private spaces, typically Venetian, e.g. the courtyards, small squares (nos. 3, 7, 42, 58, 85, 87), and the gardens (extremely numerous, even though often tiny or hidden by high walls, nos. 32, 34, 46, 53, 55, 61, 63, 66, 69, 70, 74, 77, 84), to have an idea of the care with which this domestic architecture was planned.

Small houses, then, but well designed, functional and hygienic (the ground floor was only rarely inhabited). From a study of this architecture of Venice a model of construction can be deduced which, while sometimes employing common traditional features (the façade divided vertically in three parts, for example), differs from the pattern of the more important buildings - i.e. the palaces on the Grand Canal. It is another Venice that we see, when we examine these buildings, more genuine, and one that can be restored more easily.

After all, Venice is not composed solely of great monuments, but, as Alvise Cornaro wrote four centuries ago, it is just "the numberless houses and dwellings of the citizens which go to make up the city".

Egle Renata Trincanato

Venice, June, 1978

(*) Published by Edizioni del Milione, Milan, 1948.

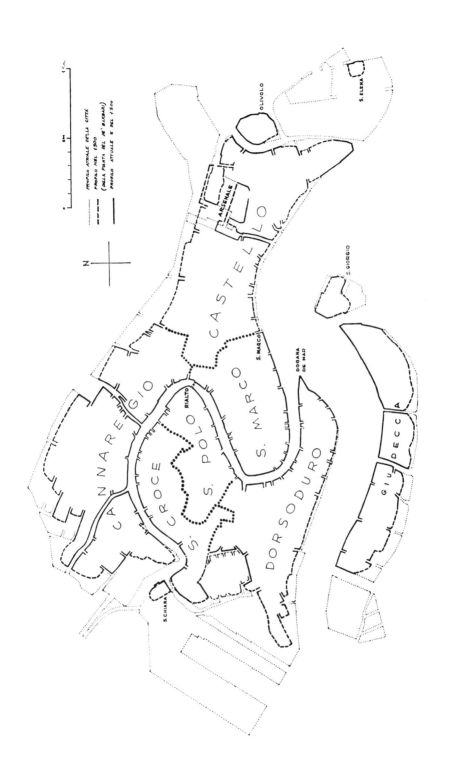

PROFILO ATTUALE DELLA CITTÀ

PROFILO NEL 1500
(DALLA PIANTA DEL DE' BARBARI)

PROFILO ATTUALE E NEL 1500

CANNAREGIO

S. CROCE

S. POLO

RIALTO

S. MARCO

CASTELLO

ARSENALE

OLIVOLO

S. ELENA

S. GIORGIO

DOGANA DE MAR

DORSODURO

GIUDECCA

S. CHIARA

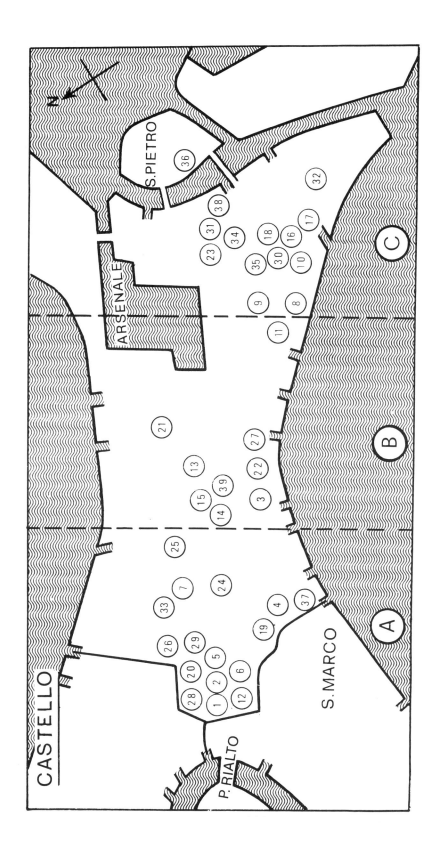

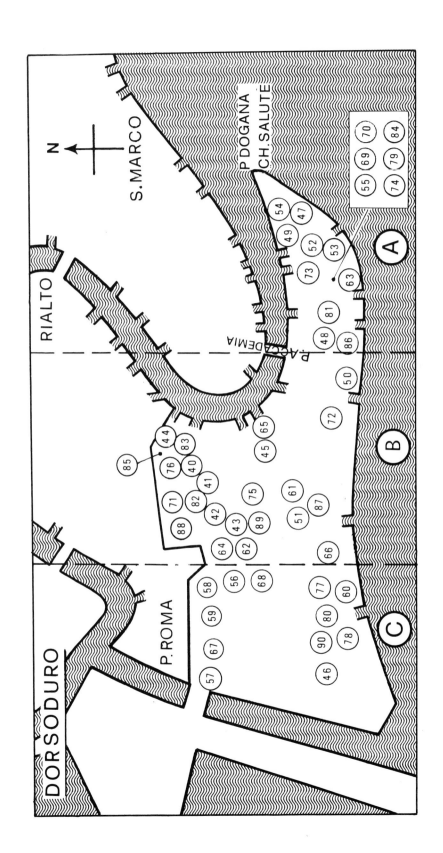

CASTELLO

NOTE

Each building dealt with includes the following practical information for the visitors:

- the number of the building in the two "Sestieri" (quarters) of Venice illustrated: Castello (**Cst.**) and Dorsoduro (**Dd.**). The Castello quarter contains 6828 numbers, beginning at S. Pietro di Castello. The Dorsoduro quarter contains 3964 beginning at the Punta della Dogana near the Church of the Salute;

- the name of the street, square, courtyard, etc. in which the building stands, followed by the name of the best known street or square nearest to it (this indication is in brackets);

- the number of the motorboat line (**M.**) with the name of the nearest stop;

- the reference number of section (**A, B** or **C**) of the plan (e.g. **p.**) of the area in which the building is situated. These plans are to be found at the beginning of the book.

It should be pointed out that the author's drawings are sometimes a reconstruction of the building in its original form, not an indication of its present state.

1 **Cst. 5691-5705** / **Salizzada S. Lio (Campo S. Bartolomeo)** / **M. 1 and 2 - Rialto** / **p. A.** Rare example of small 13th - 14th-century palace, developed in a vertical direction. Shop on the ground floor, mullioned window on first floor (with Ravenna-type capitals). The arch over the alley perhaps suggests the existence of a similar building on the opposite side.

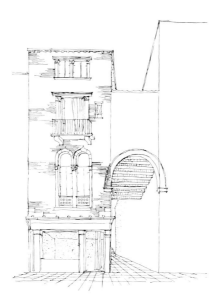

2 **Cst. 5662-72** / **Salizzada S. Lio (Campo S. Bartolomeo)** / **M. 1 and 2 - Rialto** / **p. A.** Small 13th century palace. The mullioned window on the right (with chalice-shaped capitals) was perhaps repeated on the left-hand side. The mullioned windows on the second floor, with architrave, are apparently original. The building was probably two houses built in the form of a tower, similar to the previous one.

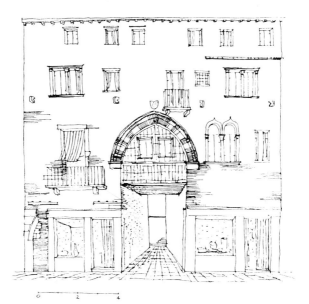

3 Cst. 3709-14 / **Corte del Papa (Calle della Pietà - Campo della Bragora)** / **M. 1 and 2 - S. Zaccaria** / **p. B.** Small palace with remains of eleventh-century work (bricked-up doorway in porch, arched-shaped shutters overlooking the internal courtyard, archway on the canal). Three-part mullioned window was rebuilt in the 16th century, with capitals dating from the 13th or 14th century. This is a tall, closed-in building, similar to the previous ones.

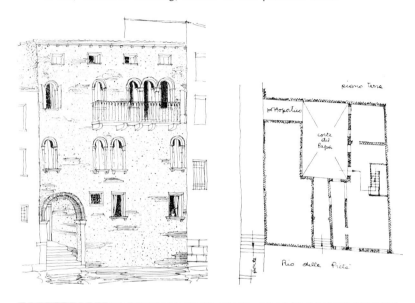

4 Cst. 4489 / **Calle Cavanella (S. Provolo)** / **M. 1 and 2 - S. Zaccaria** / **p. A.** 14th-century house with façade overlooking the courtyard with loggia and architrave; a little-known type which was probably rather common, in which wood, used for the horizontal support, was often elegantly decorated, and mixed well with the tall slim stone columns giving vertical support.

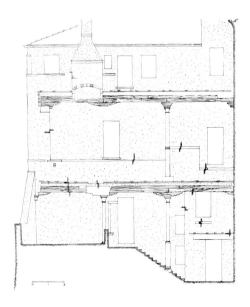

5

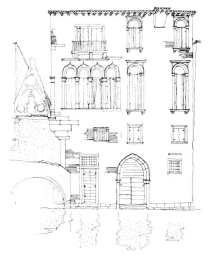

**Cst. 5729-64 / Calle del Paradiso
(Salizzada S. Lio / Rio S. M. Formosa) / M. 1 and 2 - Rialto / p. A.**
One of the most typical alleyways
of medieval Venice. Two long parallel rows of houses: shops on the
ground floor (stone pillars and
wooden architraves) butresses sup-
porting the upper floors (15th century?). Gothic archways close the
alleyway at either end (14th century). Towards Salizzada S. Lio the
whole building seems to have been
renovated during the 16th - 17th
centuries. The house on the rio di
S. M. Formosa contains features
dating from 12th - 14th centuries.

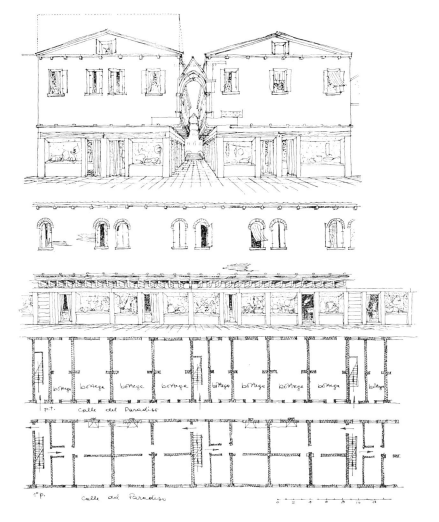

6   **Cst. 5071-76 / Salizzada S. Lio (Campo S. Bartolomeo) / M. 1 and 2 - Rialto / p. A.** Interesting example of a group of 15th-century houses with shops on the ground floor. On the first floor gothic mullioned windows with alternately one and two lights. The coat-of-arms of the Gradenigo family is visible on the façade.

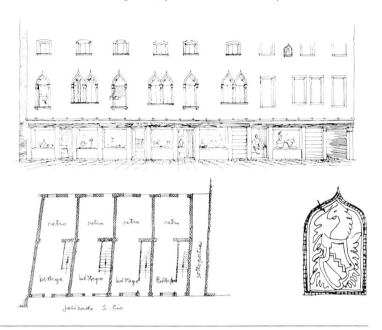

7   **Cst. 6267-81A / Corte Bottera (Fond. Felzi - Campo SS. Giovanni e Paolo) / M. 5 - Fondamente Nuove / p. A.** Of the 12th - 13th century buildings there remain the arched doorway and probably the outside staircase (partly rebuilt). Near the entrance to the Corte stands a porchway with 14th-century columns.

8 Casa della Marinarezza / Cst. 1411-68 / Corte Colonne or Schiavona (Via Garibaldi / Riva dei Sette Martiri) / M. 1 - Arsenale or Giardini / p. C. An extremely interesting example of group-residences built for a particular social aim - a foundation belonging to the Procuratoria di Citra and granted free to sailors who had distinguished themselves for their services to the Republic (this charitable institution dates from 1335). They consist of 3 parallel blocks of 3 storeys - a total of 55 houses: they can be clearly seen in the de' Barbari plan. In 1645-61 the block with two arches overlooking the basin was added. The jambs of the mullioned windows are in carved stone: chimney stacks divide up the façade. It is interesting to see that in the de' Barbari plan, towards the rio della Tana, there are two other terraced blocks, closed at either end by a crenellated wall - probably another charitable foundation which has since been rebuilt (in the present Corte Nuova there remain the old well-heads).

9 **Cst. 1980-82 and 2018-26 / Calle dei Preti (via Garibaldi) / M. 1 and 5 - Arsenale / p. C.** Fifteenth-century terraced houses similar to those just described under 8. they can be seen on the plan of de' Barbari. The top floor was added later in the 17th century.

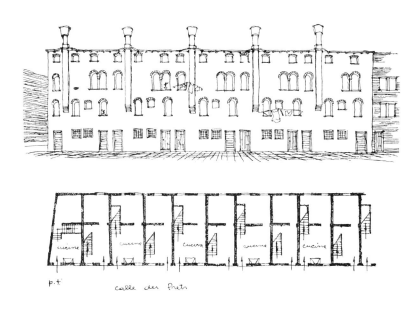

p.t'

calle dei Preti

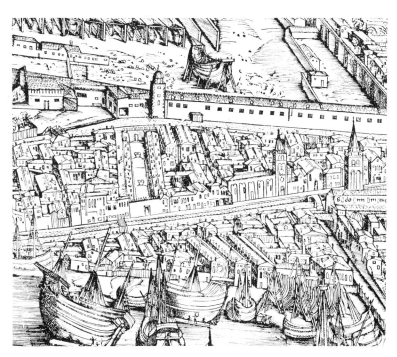

10 Cst. 1164-69 / **Calle Sarasin (Secco Marina)** / **M. 1 - Giardini** / **p. C.**
Terraced houses probably dating from 15th century. On the first
floor mullioned windows with one and two lights, and brick arched
lintels (columns with smooth chalice-shaped capitals) c.f. Calle dei
Preti, 9.

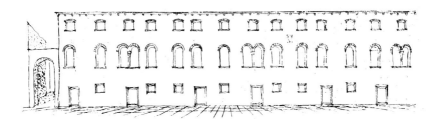

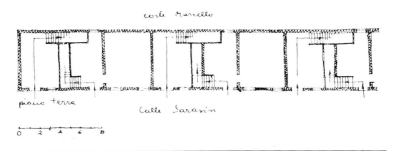

11 Cst. 1581 / **Via Garibaldi** / **M. 1 - Arsenale - 5. Tana** / **p. B.**
Elegant example of minor architecture - in its outline, its placing
of windows, and in its decorative motifs. The third floor was added
in the 17th century. Each floor has its own staircase.

12 **Palazzetto Gussoni / Cst. 5601 / Calle della Fava and Rio della Fava (Salizzada S. Lio) / M. 1 and 2 - Rialto / p. A.** Extremely ornate façade typical of the Lombardo school (Church of the Miracoli, Palazzo Dario). Asymmetric in design, overhang on the left. Traces of an earlier gothic construction can be seen: the courtyard has a portico on two sides, and a hall giving onto the canal. The 18th-century staircase has a decorative balustrade in wrought iron.

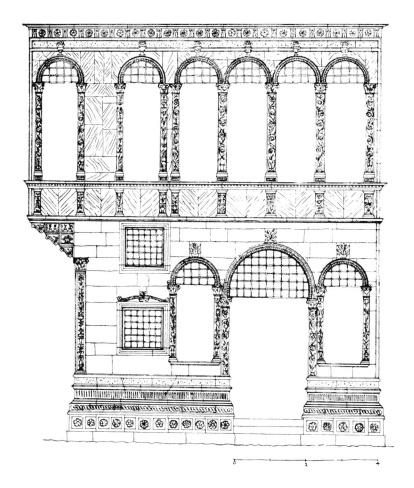

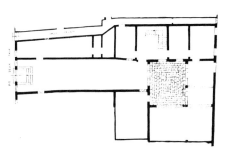

13 Cst. 3044-7 / **Calle dell'Olio (S. Francesco della Vigna)** / **M. 5 - Celestia** / **p. B.** Small 15th-century palace later transformed into modest flats. The façade facing the courtyard is picturesque, framed by the two chimney stacks.

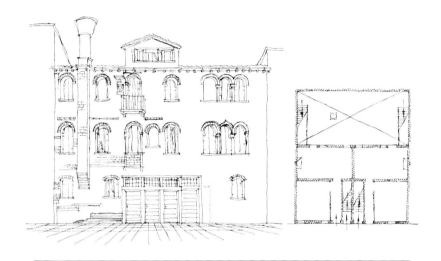

14 Cst. 3305-9 / **Salizzada dei Greci (S. Giorgio dei Greci)** / **M. 1 and 2 - S. Zaccaria** / **p. B.** Typical, well-preserved example of a sixteenth-century house with shops on the ground floor. The central part of the façade, without windows, corresponds to the two staircases inside.

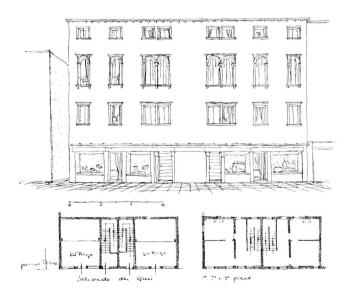

15 Cst. 3245 / **Calle dei Furlani** (S. Giorgio degli Schiavoni) / **M. 1 and 2 - S. Zaccaria** / **p. B.** Characteristic sixteenth-century Venetian house with windows placed symmetrically round the first-floor mullioned window with three lights. The interior plan has been preserved. There are two staircases, one for the first floor and one for the two upper floors which form a single flat.

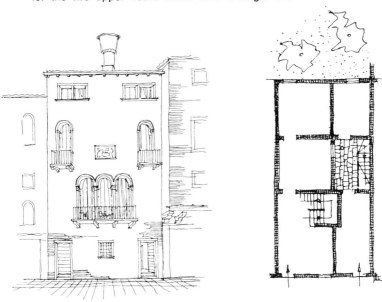

16 Cst. 519 / **Corte Soldà** (Secco Marina, Fond. S. Giuseppe) / **M. 1 - Giardini** / **p. C.** Small Renaissance palace with the date 1560 on a plaque. The façade is well-preserved, and the four-light mullioned window on the first floor still has its original wrought-iron parapet. The interior plan has undergone alterations.

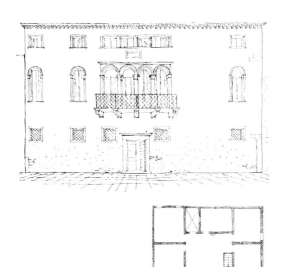

17   **Cst. 925-27 / Fondamenta S. Giuseppe / M. 1 - Giardini / p. C.**
Typical example of minor architecture in Venice at the turn of the
16th-17th centuries for the clarity with which the interior divisions
can be seen, and for the good design of the stone jambs and
lintels of the windows on the first floor.

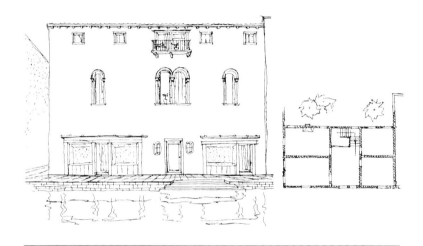

18   **Cst. 1036-37 / Calle delle Ancore (Secco Marina) / M. 1 - Giardini /
p. C.** Two two-storeyed houses make up this building; from the
façade the plain, rational distribution of the rooms can be seen.

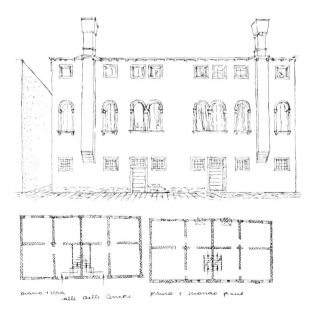

19 **Cst. 4419** / **Ponte del Rimedio (Calle Larga S. Marco)** / **M. 1 and 2 - S. Marco** / **p. A.** Important example of a façade designed solely as a background for a fresco (attributed to Tintoretto) of which only a few traces remain on the top storey. Without the fresco, the design appears unbalanced.

20 **Cst. 5891-5903** / **Campo S. Marina (S. Maria Formosa)** / **M. 1 and 2 - Rialto** / **p. A.** These 16th-century houses consist of two blocks separated by an alleyway with high arches joining the two sides, thus forming a single façade. Rational distribution of rooms: the plan, including that of the chimneys is perfectly symmetrical.

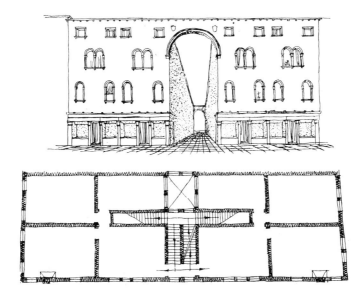

21 Cst. 3059 / **Campo S. Ternita (S. Francesco della Vigna)** / **M. 5 - Celestia** / **p. B.** Pleasant 16th-century house with a horizontal design; the central part has an important three-part mullioned window and a private bridge, while above the roof line stands an elegant dormer window with its tympanum.

22 Cst. 3723-31 / **Campo Bandiera e Moro o della Bragora (Riva degli Schiavoni)** / **M. 1 and 2 - S. Zaccaria** / **p. B.** From the façade of this group of small houses dating from the seventeenth century, the plan of the three houses each containing two flats, can be clearly seen. The flats are rationally placed, exploiting the space well. Elegant iron balconies adorn the centre of each flat.

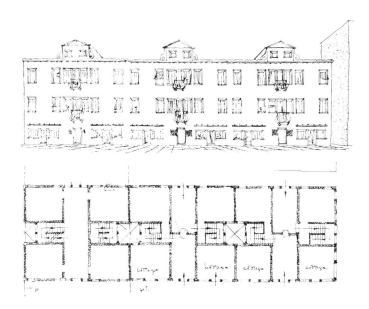

23 Cst. 329-30 / **Campo Ruga (S. Pietro di Castello)** / **M. 1 - Giardini** / **p. C.** Small well-designed and well-preserved seventeenth-century palace, with 3-part mullioned window on one side, following the traditional asymmetrical plan. The original interior plan has undergone changes. A portico, running the whole length of the building leads to a courtyard.

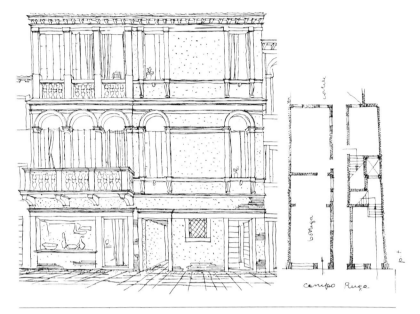

24 Cst. 4860-62 / **Ramo Grimani in Ruga Giuffa (S. M. Formosa)** / **M. 1 and 2 - S. Zaccaria** / **p. A.** Well-preserved 17th-century palace, bordered by rusticated corners, with a tall, severe air. The interior plan has remained unchanged. The central staircase is exploited scenographically in the baroque manner.

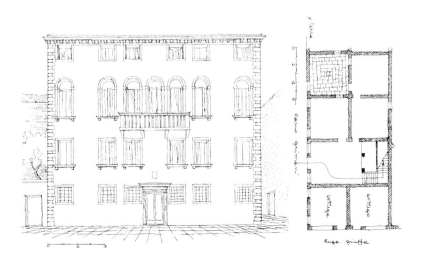

25 Cst. 6379 / **Rio della Tetta (Calle Lunga S. M. Formosa)** / **M. 5 -
Fondamente Nuove** / **p. A.** Small 17th-century house, tall and narrow:
below a portico giving onto the canal. Windows in line towards the
outside edges of the façade, leaving uninterrupted wall in the centre
(traces of frescoes).

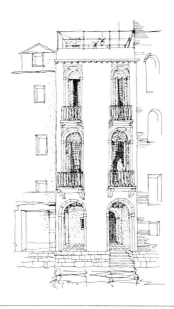

26 Palazzetto Dandolo / Cst. 6824-26 / **Fondamenta Dandolo (Campo
SS. Giovanni e Paolo)** / **M. 5 - Fondamente Nuove** / **p. A.** Small
17th-century palace which is well-preserved both as regards façade
and interior plan. The two chimney stacks form part of the symmetrical prospect in the manner of minor Venetian architecture. This
building is reproduced in Canaletto's painting « Il Rio dei Mendi-
canti ».

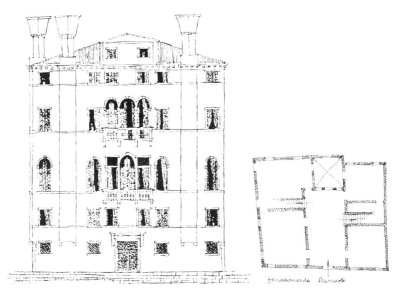

27 **Cst. 3983-91 / Campo della Pescaria (Riva degli Schiavoni) / M. 1 and 2 - S. Zaccaria / p. B.** Two houses joined by an archway over which the third floor is unified, unlike the first two (this is often found in early buildings). The whole is clearly 17th-century, with carefully-distanced single windows. The staircase serves six flats, two on each floor.

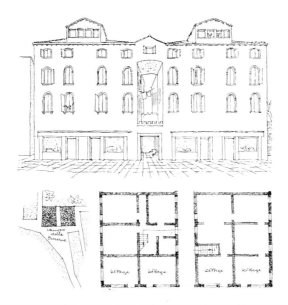

28 **Cst. 5943-46 / Calle del Piombo, Calle Martinengo and Calle del Frutarol (Campo S. Marina) / M. 1 and 2 - Rialto / p. A.** Typical unpretentious late 17th-century house overlooking Calle del Frutarol: on the ground floor supported by 5 pillars, and above the windows are rhythmically spaced between two imposing chimney stacks.

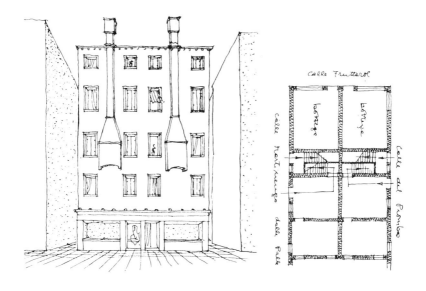

29 **Cst. 5867 / Borgoloco Molmenti (Campo S. M. Formosa) / M. 1 and 2 - Rialto / p. A.** Late 16th- or early 17th-century building, this small palace has its façade overlooking the canal designed in a tri-partite plan by a sure hand. The side with overhanging wooden beams, repeats the lines of white stone from the façade, is interrupted only by the windows on the stairs.

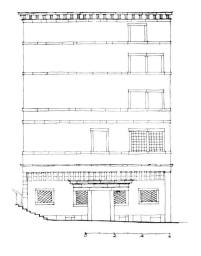

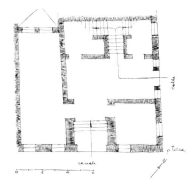

30 **Cst. 1094-98** / **Calle delle Furlane (Secco Marina)** / **M. 1 - Giardini** /
p. C. This alleyway, originally probably inhabited by people from
Friuli, shows traces of mountain houses in its modest 17th-century
dwellings (large chimney stacks, square windows, overhanging roof
to the attic window) - these are quite different from the usual
Venetian models. Each house contains two tiny flats, and has two
separate entrances, one on each side of the building.

31 **Cst. 327-28** / **Campo Ruga (S. Pietro di Castello)** / **M. 1 - Giardini** /
p. C. This 17th-century palace was probably built for two shop-
keepers or boat-owners (there are two separate entrances and two
shops on the ground floor); it has a lively, provincial robust air.

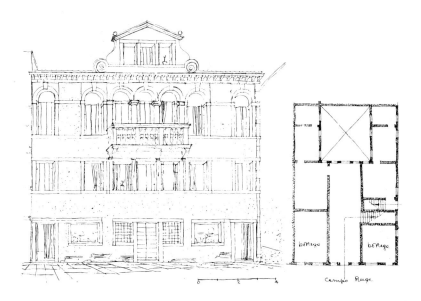

32 **Cst. 831-32** / **Paludo S. Antonio (S. Giuseppe)** / **M. 1 - Giardini** / **p. C.** This pair of houses for fishermen dating from the 17th century once lay at the extreme edge of the town. Even though they are exceedingly modest, they have a clear, simple design.

piano terra   primo piano

33 **Palazzetto Cocco** / **Cst. 6165** / **Calle Cocco del Remer (S. M. Formosa)** / **M. 1 and 2 - S. Zaccaria** / **p. A.** This 18th-century palazzo is typical of the symmetrical spacing of the rooms on the façade. Example of richness of the lively baroque style: an archway from the calle corresponds to the archway of the entrance on the canal.

34 **Cst. 318-20** / **Calle Maraffoni - Calle delle Ole (Canale di S. Pietro)** / **M. 1 - Giardini** / **p. C.** These two small houses (since demolished) each had a garden (also destroyed). The first one consisted of a pair of white houses overlooking the canal. The whole group has been replaced by an anonymous modern building.

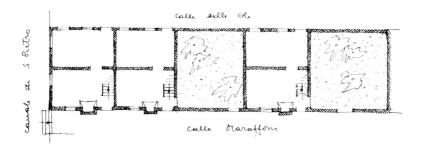

35   Cst. 458-461 / **Fondamenta del Rio della Tana (Via Garibaldi)** /
M. 1 - Giardini / **p. C.** This interesting group of terraced houses
bears witness to the maturity that modest buiding had reached in the
18th century. Standardised interior plans and harmonious rhythmical
placing of windows and doors on the façade.

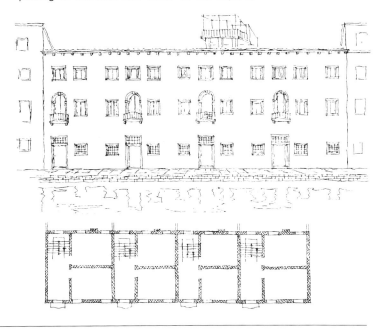

36   Cst. 54-57 / **Fondamenta Quintavalle (S. Pietro di Castello)** / **M. 1 -
Giardini** / **p. C.** Two pairs of houses, each with its own dormer
window and front door. The interior plan reveals the same simple
scheme.

37 **Cst. 4612-25 / Calle delle Rasse / M. 1 and 2 - S. Zaccaria / p. A.**
This building is one of the first examples of multi-storey houses
built for letting in 1737 by Antonio Visetti for the Michiel family.
It is an interesting attempt to construct rational groups of dwelling
units.

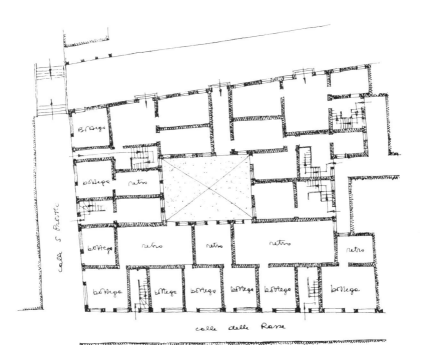

38 Cst. 227-30 / Rio di S. Anna, Calle S. Anna (Via Garibaldi) / M. 1 - Giardini / p. C. 18th-century terraced houses, the façade overlooking the canal was once marked by large chimney stacks (now partly destroyed): the windows are in pairs. In the calle one- and two-light windows alternate with each other; there are two different interior plans.

39 Cst. 3274-80 / Calle dei Furlani (S. Giorgio degli Schiavoni) / M. 1 and 2 - S. Zaccaria / p. B. This 18th-century house built for letting has its façade divided up by the repeated horizontal lines of stone, windows in pairs, and two central balconies on the 2nd and 3rd floors: it is similar to the building in Calle delle Rasse (n. 37). Its interior plan is well preserved: central courtyard.

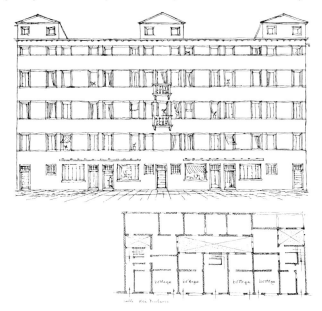

DORSODURO

40 **Dd. 3393 / Rio di Cà Foscari (S. Margherita) / M. 1 - Cà Rezzonico /
p. B.** A series of small arches with tall corbels (incorporated in a
later building) interrupted by an wider arch in the centre which
probably served as the entrance from the canal leading to the
warehouses and the courtyard of this 13th-century building.

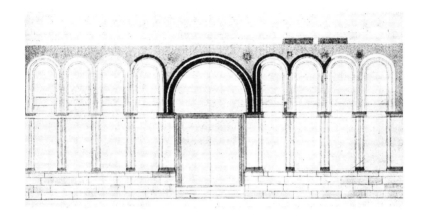

41 **Dd. 3413-25 / Corte del Fontego (Campo S. Margherita) / M. 1 -
Cà Rezzonico / p. B.** Portico and six arches, five of which have
been walled - in, probably formed part of the courtyard of a private
13th-century house, now incorporated in a 17th- or 18th-century
building. The capitals are bell-shaped with leaves at the corners.

42 **Casa Foscolo Corner** / **Dd. 2920-35** / **Campo S. Margherita** / **M. 1 - Cà Rezzonico** / **p. B.** These buildings (attributed to Celega) probably acquired their present form between the end of the 14th and the early 15th-century: the original building fabric was wholly or partly rebuilt - the doorway of Casa Foscolo is a tangible witness of this early building - this cannot be dated later than the 13th century (perhaps even the 12th), considering the elegance with which the architraved doorway is sculptured in red Verona marble, and the Byzantine refinement of the decoration in brickwork in the lunette above the door.

Casa Foscolo Corner

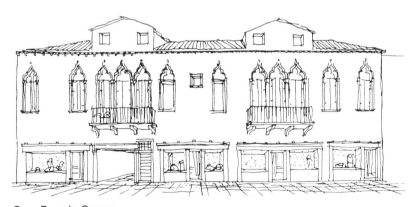

Casa Foscolo Corner
(left)

43 Dd. 2945-62 / Campo S. Margherita / M. 1 - Cà Rezzonico / p. B.
Two adjacent 14th-century houses, the left-hand one has the façade
divided into three parts. The ground floor is typical - an uninterrupted
series of architraves; the mezzanine floor has small square windows.
The projecting roof of the right-hand palace is unusual.

44 Dd. 3855 / Crosera S. Pantalon (Cà Foscari) / M. 1 - S. Tomà / p. B.
Small 14th-century house with a three-part mullioned window with
Venetian Gothic arches in brickwork on the façade. To this same
period also belongs the window with iron grill corresponding to the
former staircase. The second-floor windows are later. The interior
plan has been altered somewhat, but not in its main features; on
the ground floor there is the shop in front, the back room and a
kitchen (probably used as an old inn, as at present). On the right-
hand corner there is a capital, once perhaps part of a side
archway over the alley.

45 Dd. 2779-80 / **Calle del Traghetto and Rio Malpaga (S. Barnaba)** /
M. 1 - Cà Rezzonico / **p. B.** The façade overlooking the rio of this
late 14th-century house is similar to the one in the calle which has
a shop on the ground floor. The adjacent house originally had a
similar plan.

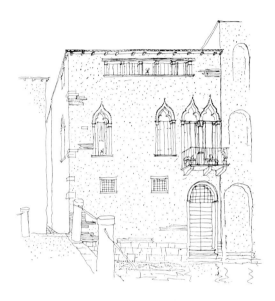

46 **Ospizio Zuane Contarini** / **Dd. 2209-10** / **Fondamenta delle Terese**
(S. Nicolò dei Mendicoli) / **M. 5 - S. Basilio** / **p. C.** Picturesque
group of buildings of different architectural styles, which is given
order and equilibrium by the horizontal line of the wall which
surrounds them. The gothic construction (14th century) in the middle
is still used as an almshouse.

47 Palazzetto Costantini / Dd. 70 / Rio terrà dei Catecumeni / M. 1 - Salute / p. A. Early 15th-century building: the portico with its wooden architrave (14th century) originally stood on the edge of the canal which was filled-in during the 19th century. The stone doorway in the wall has the same gothic characteristics as those of the 4 single windows on the façade, with lobed arches, terminating in a vertex.

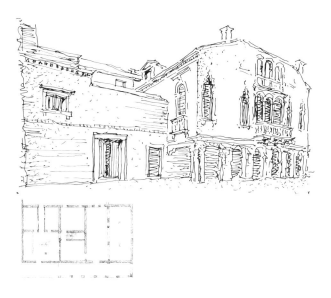

48 Dd. 843 / Piscina Venier (S. Agnese) / M. 1 and 2 - Accademia / p. A. Small 15th-century palace, characteristic of Venetian architecture of the period: spacing between the windows is irregular, the ground-floor windows are independent from those of the upper floors: entrance and ground-floor windows placed round a large, elegant chimney stack.

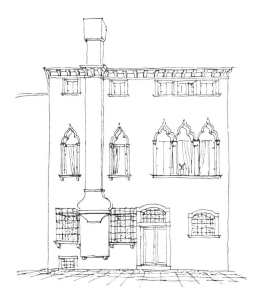

49 Dd. 153-8 / **Calle Lanza** / **M. 1 - Salute** / **p. A.** These small 15th-century houses, part of a large group, perhaps forming almshouses, built by the Lanza family (their coat-of-arms can be seen on the façade) do not yet show the symmetry typical of the Renaissance period. Arched windows with brick lintels. These houses were restored in 1960 under the auspices of Italia Nostra.

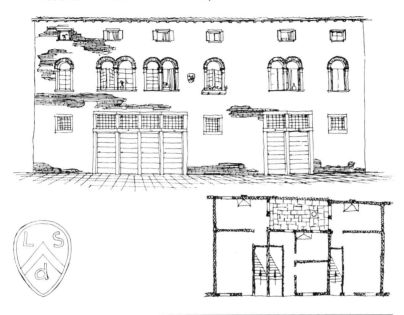

50 Dd. 929 / **Zattere** / **M. 1 - Zattere, 1 and 2 - Accademia** / **p. B.** The 16th-century style of tri-partite division of the façade can be clearly seen: it rises airily above a 15th-century portico, supported by slender stone columns corbels and robust architraves of wood. This portico was used as a public right of way when the fondamenta was built in 1519.

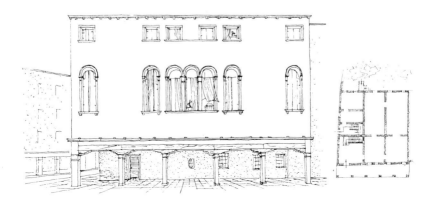

51 Dd. 1590-91 / **Ponte dell'Avogaria (S. Sebastiano)** / **M. 5 - S. Basilio** / **p. B.** Small palace dating from the late 15th century with elegant details of styling: the motif of the 3-part mullioned window with rounded arches and balcony on the second floor is repeated in the almost square windows with stone architraves on the mezzanine floor. The ground floor and the larger chimney underwent alterations in the 17th century.

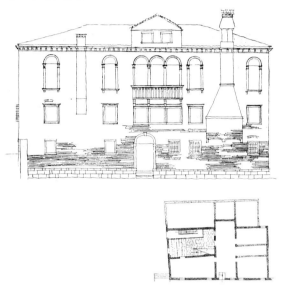

52 Dd. 212 / **Fondamenta Ca' Balà** / **M. 1 - Salute** / **p. A.** Sixteenth-century house with a large hall on the first floor which acted as living room and passage-way onto which the other rooms give. The windows right at the edge of the walls are balanced by the vertical line of the chimney stack. The house was once covered with frescoes and there are still some traces visible.

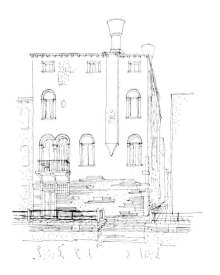

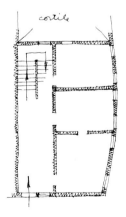

53 **Dd. 222 / Fondamenta Ca' Balà / M. 1 - Salute / p. A.** The main feature of this 16th-century façade is a striking 7-part mullioned window taking up more than half the width of the house, in the medieval Venetian tradition. The interior plan follows the external features exactly: two orthogonal flights of stairs at the end of the ground-floor entrance hall.

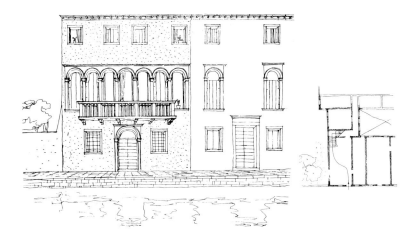

54 **Dd. 141 / Rio terrà del Spezier (Catecumeni) / M. 1 - Salute / p. A.** The two floors of this late 16th-century house stand over the horizontal space of the portico. The non-symmetrical spacing of the windows reflects the interior plan.

55 **Dd. 475 / Rio terrà S. Vio / M. 1 and 2 - Accademia / p. A.**
Small 16th-century house which has suffered much alteration. Originally it was probably the end of a series of terraced houses. The
remains of the 15th-century wall which perhaps barred the alleyway
or courtyard between two lines of these symmetrical houses, in
the Venetian tradition.

56 **Dd. 2511-14 / Fondamenta Rossa and Corte Bonazza (Fondamenta
Cereri) / M. 1 and 2 - Piazzale Roma / p. C.** The tri-partite division
of the façade of this house overlooking corte Bonazza emphasises
the plastic function of the chimney stacks which separate the
groups of windows: on the ground floor, doors and pairs of small
windows alternate.

57 Corte delle Procuratie (Fondamenta delle Procuratie and Fondamenta Cereri) / M. 1 and 2 - Piazzale Roma / p. C. Between the
Fondamenta delle Procuratie and Fondamenta Cereri up to the
early 19th century, there existed an interesting group of buildings
consisting of about 70 tiny terraced houses, dating from the
16th century: 4 blocks of buidings overlooking two long parallel
courtyards (similar to those of the Marinarezza, no. 8) They were
built with a bequest made in 1502 by Filippo Tron, and the houses
were occupied by poor families "amore dei"; the property was
administered by the Procuratori de Ultra (hence the present-day
name of the fondamenta). Later on this site terraces of modest
houses were constructed. (c.f. nos. 58, 59, 67).

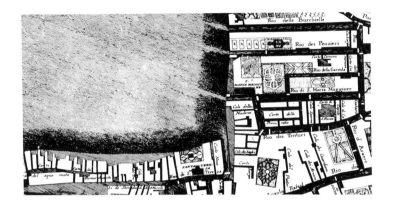

58 Dd. 2490-2503 / Corte S. Marco (Fondamenta Cereri) / M. 1 and 2 -
Piazzale Roma / p. C. 24 small houses, built in 1529 with a bequest
of Pietro Olivieri made to the members of the Scuola di S. Marco
(Guild). They were partly rebuilt in 1599 (inscription on a well-head).
These are examples of seventeenth-century working-class housing,
as can be seen from the perfect symmetry both of the plan and
the elevations.

59 **Dd. 2468-71 / Calle Cappello (Fondamenta Cereri) / M. 1 and 2 - Piazzale Roma / p. C.** This 17th-century building, consisting of two blocks (each of which contains two flats, one over the other) exemplifies an interesting type of staircase (intersecting ramps, like those of Leonardo) which permits access to 2 flats on different floors, making use of the same stair-well, with alternating flights.

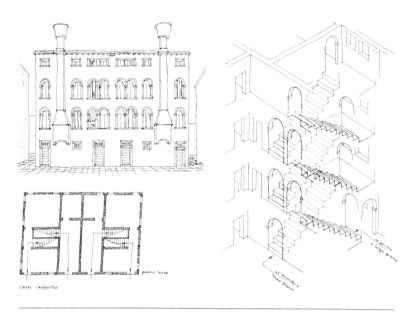

60 **Dd. 1511-22 / Campo S. Basilio and Fondamenta Zattere / M. 5 - S. Basilio / p. C.** Seventeenth-century house for letting with identical elevations overlooking the Campo and the other overlooking the Zattere, with the traditional style of the triptych. Interior plan is carefully organised round a small central courtyard which came into fashion at this period and enabled the maximum space available to be exploited. Eight staircases serve as many flats (four on each storey) from the mezzanine to the attic floor.

61   **Dd. 2714-15 / Calle Lunga S. Barnaba / M. 1 - Cà Rezzonico / p. B.** 17th-century house with wooden buttresses: large areas of blank wall between the few windows. The original plan is still legible: the transverse staircases divide the flats in two symmetrical parts

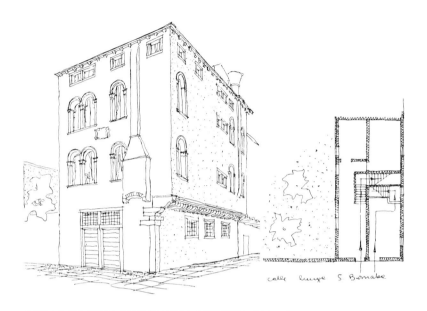

62   **Dd. 2967-8 / Calle del Forno (Campo S. Margherita) / M. 1 - Cà Rezzonico / p. B.** Another 17th-century house with overhanging wooden buttressing (the date on the plaque is 1684). The style of single windows close together (instead of 2-part mullioned windows) is typical of this period. All the windows are rectangular: the buttresses themselves are perhaps earlier than the rest of the house. The interior plan has undergone alterations.

63 **Dd. 436-8 / Ramo calle dietro gli Incurabili (S. Vio) / M. 1 and 2 - Accademia / p. A.** A pair of houses dated 1608 (one built later above the other) exemplifying all the characteristics of the period: tri-partite mullioned windows with architrave, robust chimneys, small doors with windows above them, and at either side, windows are framed in flat stone.

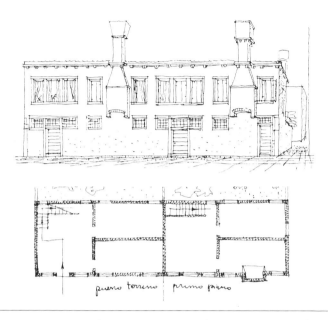

64 **Palazzo Marcorà / Dorsoduro 3448-9 / Fondamenta Bembo o del Malcanton (Campo S. Margherita) / M. 1 - Cà Rezzonico / p. B.** Typical 17th-century square façade, divided horizontally into three clearly-marked parts: the two lower floors, the second floor, marked by an upper cornice above the windows, and the square windows of the top floor immediately beneath the roof cornice. The façade was once frescoed.

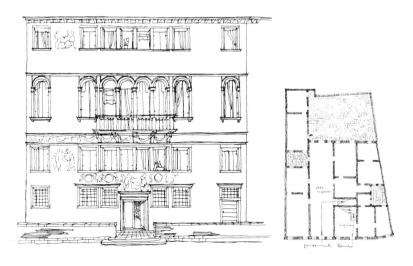

65 **Dd. 2794 / Fondamenta del Traghetto sul Canal Grande (S. Barnaba) / M. 1 - Cà Rezzonico / p. B.** Interesting façade in the baroque style: the main floor (second) stands high above the two lower ones, and the crowning of the building includes the square windows of the top storey as part of the frieze. The original asymmetrical interior plan has undergone alterations.

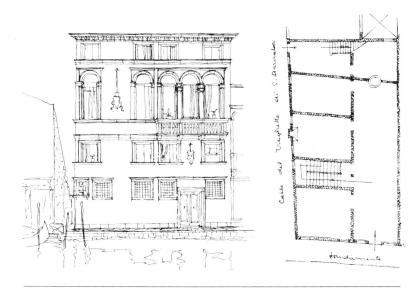

66 **Dd. 1439-41 / Rio Terrà Ognissanti (S. Trovaso) / M. 5 - Zattere, 1 and 2 - Accademia / p. B.** Typical 17th-century façade which once overlooked the canal (now filled in) and still has the canal entrance. There are two flats - one on each floor - the windows are placed close together, all uniform. The building is marked out by the two chimney stacks and the three attics, all with dormer windows.

67 Dd. 2410-30 / **Fondamenta Cereri and Fondamenta delle Procuratie** / **M. 1 and 2 - Piazzale Roma** / **p. C.** This group of houses dating from the late 16th or early 17th century consists of two blocks joined by arches at either end. It is interesting because it unites in the same group of buildings elegant flats (at either end of the blocks) together with modest dwellings in the middle. Good use is made of the interior space, and staircases of the Leonardo type lead up to each flat.

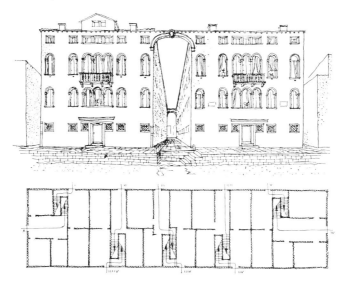

68 **Palazzo Vendramin** / **Dorsoduro 3462** / **Fondamenta Foscarini (Carmini)** / **M. 1 - Cà Rezzonico** / **p. C.** Building remarkable for the vertical quality, emphasised by the tall narrow windows, one above the other, connected by cornices, as though they were hanging, in the late baroque style; in contrast, the ininterrupted wall on the ground floor.

69 **Dd. 444-445 / Calle Navarro and Calle Incurabili (S. Vio) / M. 1 and 2 - Accademia / p. A.** This house, consisting of two flats one above the other, over a ground floor of entrance halls and storerooms, exemplifies the late 17th-century style of architecture. Alternating staircases leading to the two flats.

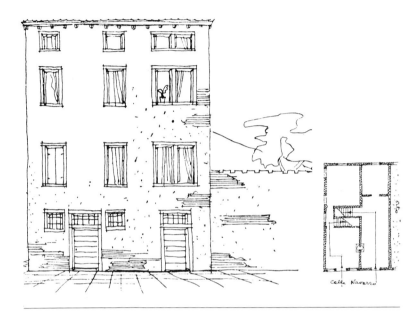

70 **Dd. 432-47 / Rio terrà S. Vio and Calle degli Incurabili / M. 1 and 2 - Accademia / p. A.** The façade of this house dated 1681 (date engraved on each corner of the building) beneath a statuette of the risen Christ) shows all the characteristics of this period: contrasting lines marking the different storeys, running all the way round the building, square rooms and flat borders round the windows. The ground plan is rectangular in shape, absolutely symmetrical, with the staircase in the centre of each flat.

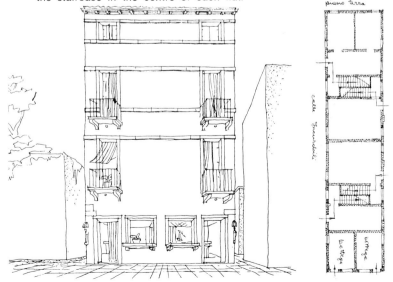

71 Palazzo Gabrielli Dolfin / Dd. 3593 / Fondamenta Malcanton (Tolentini) / M. 1 and 2 - Piazzale Roma / p. B. Interesting example of a façade showing in the late 17th-century how the traditional Venetian style, dividing the building horizontally into three parts, persisted during the baroque period.

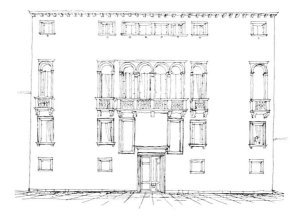

72 Squero di S. Trovaso / Dd .1097 / Campo S. Trovaso / M. 1 and 2 - Accademia / p. B. A rough over-all plan joins three separate buildings together: they form this seventeenth-century boatyard. The residential quarters are on the top floor - the long wooden balcony can be seen with its parapet. The lowest building is a shed covering the working area of the boatyard, giving onto the canal.

73 **Dd. 375** / **Fondamenta Zorzi (S. Vio)** / **M. 1 and 2 - Accademia** / **p. A.** This small house probably underwent alterations during the 17th century; well-designed windows with architraves on the first floor, 2-part mullioned window at the centre. On the ground floor, wide areas of uninterrupted wall, with a antique gothic archway in the centre. This clever design is given added interest by two complicated chimney-pots which are clearly renaissance in character.

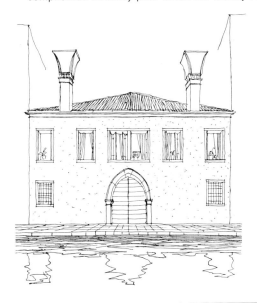

74 **Dd. 460** / **Rio terrà S. Vio** / **M. 1 and 2 - Accademia** / **p. A.** This eighteenth-century palace exemplifies all the characteristics of the traditional Venetian house: on the façade the asymmetrical design of the 3-part mullioned window corresponding to the main room, while a network of horizontal and vertical lines gives an interesting effect to the rest of the façade.

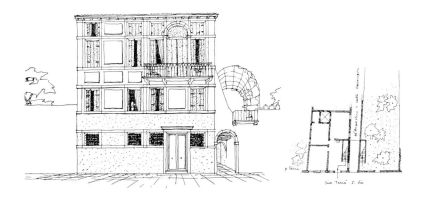

75 Dd. 3042-3 / Campo S. Margherita / M. 1 - Cà Rezzonico / p. B.
Like many eighteenth-century buildings in Venice, this small palace
repeats the usual asymmetrical design of traditional architecture.
A large 4-part mullioned window occupies half the breadth of the
façade and marks the position of the main hall. The top-storey
windows are connected by horizontal lines of stonework, creating
a frieze-effect just below the roof.

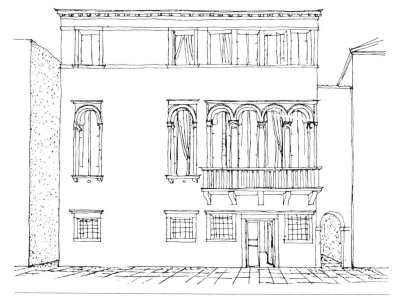

76 Palazzetto Paruta /Dd. 3721-25 / Rio di Cà Foscari (S. Pantalon) /
M. 1 - S. Tomà / p. B. The façade of this palace overlooking the
canal is probably unfinished, and exemplifies the characteristics of
barocco architecture mixed with those of the eighteenth century:
the former in the method of connecting the balconies with the
windows below, in the elongated form of the windows and in the
absence of horizontal stonework in the façade. The latter can be
seen in the substitution of single windows for the 3- and 4-part
windows previously used.

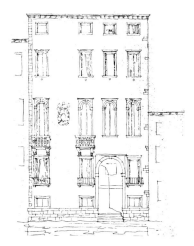

77 Dd. 2355 / **Fondamenta Barbarigo (Angelo Raffaele) / M. 5 - S. Basilio / p. C.** This eighteenth-century building has a tri-partite façade with small square windows in the first and third storeys, shops on the ground floor on either side of the entrance-way, and tall, arched windows on the second floor. The double window in the centre corresponds to a very long hall, which might point to the building being used as an old people's home.

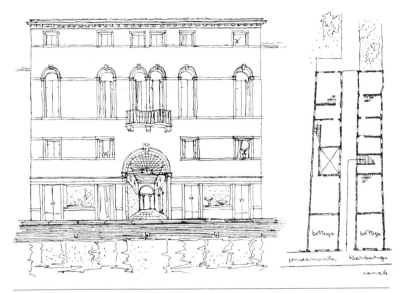

78 Dd. 1837 / **Fondamenta di Pescaria (S. Nicolò dei Mendicoli) / M. 5 - S. Basilio / p. C.** This building was designed for letting and demolished in the post-war period; it stood three storeys high in a perfectly symmetrical rectangular block, back and front, revealing a late 18th-century taste for somewhat monotonous window-spacing on all three floors; only the windows balconies over the entrances give some life to the façade, divding it into 3 separate areas.

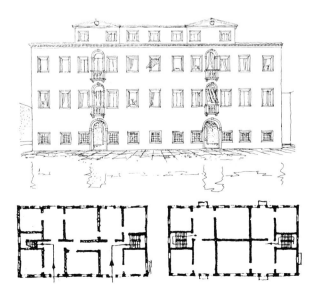

79 Dd. 512-17 / **Calle delle Mende (Rio terrà S. Vio)** / **M. 1 and 2 - Accademia** / **p. A.** These terraced houses on two floors forms one of the best examples of its kind in minor Venetian architecture of the 18th century, both due to its balance between spaces and solids and to the lively design of the whole. Here the figurative language, architraves and horizontal stonework bands, flat surrounds to the windows, achieves particularly pleasing results.

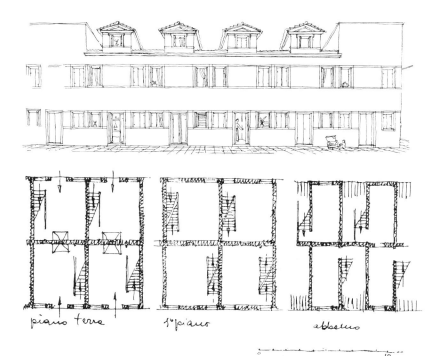

piano terra   1°piano   abbaino

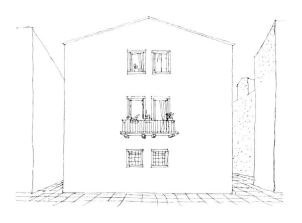

80 **Dd. 1767-69 / Fondamenta di Pescaria (Angelo Raffaele) / M. 5 - S. Basilio / p. C.** The interior plan of this house has been completely altered, but its façade exemplifies the common features of 18th-century Venetian architecture: the habit of separating windows, not grouping them together, and the tendency to mark off the storeys horizontally with narrow bands in relief.

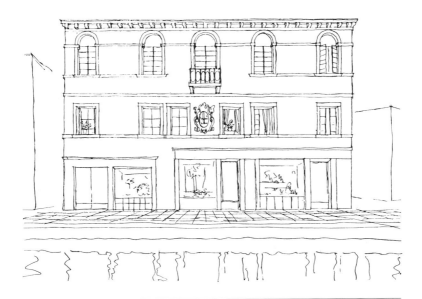

81 **Dd. 605 / Fondamenta Bragadin (Zattere) / M. 1 and 2 - Accademia, 5 - Zattere / p. A.** This small house has a pleasant 18th-century façade, with vertical interest in the centre, emphasising the main storey of the house with its central wrought-iron balcony - the sole decorative note in the rigorous severity of all the other elements of the façade. Built for the Scuola di S. Rocco.

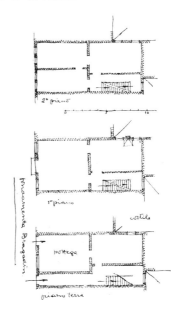

82 **Dd. 3429-30 / Campo S. Margherita / M. 1 - Cà Rezzonico / p. B.**
This lively 18th-century façade has as its main feature on the
3 upper storeys windows with stone balconies one above the other,
forming a single vertical feature. These elements frame the central
zone of the building with large areas of ininterrupted wall, particularly on the ground floor, while on the top storey the small square
windows are placed closely round the central niche containing a
15th-century statue of Santa Margherita (formerly in the church of
the same name, now a cinema).

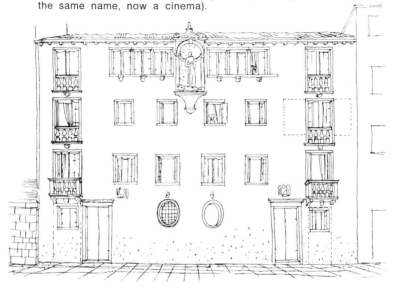

83 **Dd. 3717-18 / Rio di Cà Foscari and Campiello Angaran (S. Pantalon) / M. 1 - S. Tomà / p. B.** The façade of this pair of 18th-century
houses is marked by two large arched doorways over which two
niches are placed, giving added emphasis. The windows are in
vertical lines, rather tall and narrow, especially on the second storey.

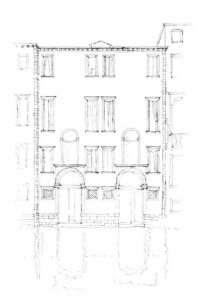

84   Dd. 532-45 / **Calle Navarro and Calle del Forno (Rio terrà S. Vio)** /
M. 1 and 2 - Accademia / p. A. This group of 16 modest houses
shows a certain originality in plan and design, although it follows
the normal scheme. Two identical blocks with two small walled
gardens, each block with 8 doors (4 on one side and 4 on the
other) corresponding to the 8 flats within. A well-designed series
of wooden staircases allows the separate flats to be independent.

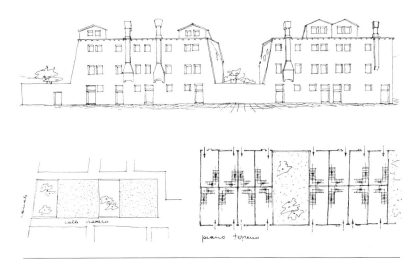

85   Dd. 3789-92 / **Corte dei Preti and rio della Scuola di S. Rocco** /
M. 1 - S. Tomà / p. B. This small house is situated in the centre
of the courtyard, and is interesting on account of some features
of its 18th-century façade. Its main characteristic is the second
storey attic in the centre of the building with a terrace on either
side.

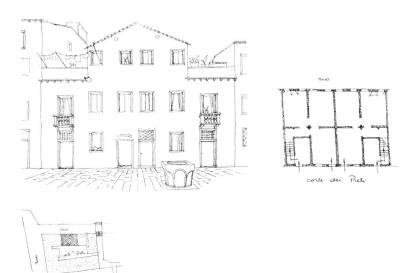

86 **Dd. 830-33 / Piscina S. Agnese / M. 1 and 2 - Accademia, 5 - Zattere / p. A.** The second storey attic of this 18th-century house is crowned by a pediment. The doors on the ground floor are arranged in pairs, leaving uninterrupted wall in the centre of the façade, and showing where the two identical houses meet. In the centre of this wall a statuette of the Madonna stands in a niche.

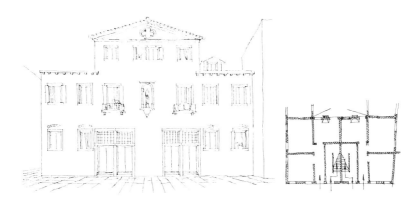

87 **Dd. 1556-65 / Calle Balastro (Fondamenta S. Basilio) / M. 5 - S. Basilio / p. B.** These early 18th-century houses — even though they are exceedingly unpretentious — exemplify, in the careful balance of wall, doors and windows, the simplicity of good design.

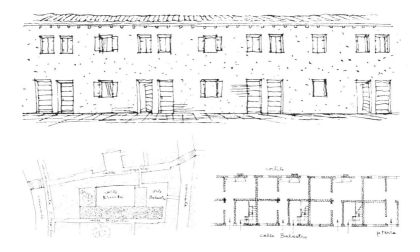

88 **Dd. 3532 / Fondamenta del Gaffaro (Tolentini) / M. 1 and 2 - Piazzale Roma / p. B.** This small 18th-century façade has 3 storeys: the central arched window seems to be out of proportion compared to the other windows, and shows the influence of Verona and Sansovino.

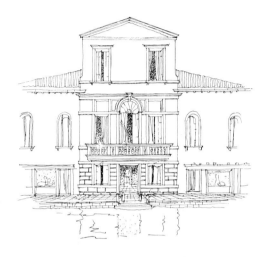

89 **Dd. 3034-35 / Campo S. Margherita / M. 1 - Cà Rezzonico / p. B.** This almshouse for poor women was founded in 1482 with a bequest of Maddalena Scrovegni (a member of the Padua family which built the church of S. Maria dell'Arena) and was rebuilt in 1762 (c.f. stone plaque on the façade). The 18th-century style can be detected in the way in which the various elements of the traditional 3-part design are combined together.

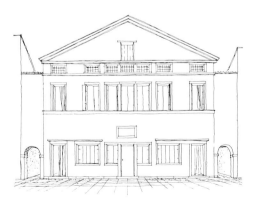 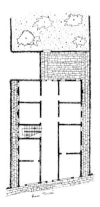

90 **Dd. 1876-91** / **Fondamenta Tron (S. Nicolò dei Mendicoli)** / **M. 5 -
S. Basilio** / **p. C.** These are extremely modest 18th-century houses
on the outskirts of the city. The façade overlooking the Fondamenta
Tron boasts 7 robust chimneys which thus constitute an important
architectural feature, given emphasis by the smallness of the square
windows on the first and second floors.

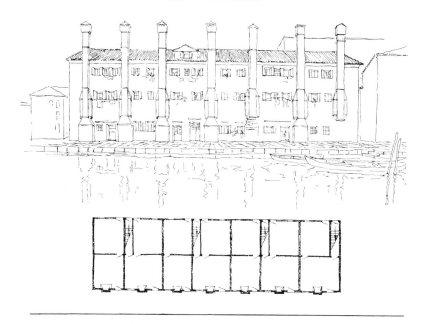

INDEX

Figures refer to item numbers

NOTES

NOTES